Whispers Of Wisdom

Quotes, Volume 1

Samer Merhi

Published by Samer Merhi, 2025.

WHISPERS OF WISDOM

First edition. April 23, 2025.

Copyright © 2025 Samer Merhi.

ISBN: 979-8231921119

Written by Samer Merhi.

Table of Contents

Introduction

In the quiet moments of reflection, wisdom whispers to the soul. **"Whispers of Wisdom"** is more than just a collection of quotes—it is a journey through life's cycles, offering insights shaped by experience, resilience, and the unbreakable spirit of Lebanon and its people.

Each page holds a carefully crafted quote, paired with a deep reflection, inviting you to pause, think, and connect with the essence of life.

This book is not meant to be read in one sitting. Let it be a companion, a source of guidance, and a reminder that every stage of life carries its own lessons. Whether you seek clarity, strength, or inspiration, may these whispers find their way to your heart and illuminate your path.

Welcome to a book that speaks to the soul—**one quote at a time.**

Chapter 1: The Power of Self-Mastery

"A healthy dose of ego is always required, as many misunderstand humbleness."

True humility is not about erasing your sense of self or diminishing your own worth. Rather, it is about the quiet confidence of knowing who you are and embracing your abilities without the need to constantly prove yourself to others. A balanced ego allows you to stand strong in your truth while still acknowledging and respecting the light in those around you. It serves as a bridge between self-respect and universal harmony, helping you navigate the delicate balance between confidence and grace. With the right amount of ego, you honor both your own value and the potential in others, creating a space where respect, strength, and humility coexist.

* * *

"Through isolation, you reach elevation."

In the sanctuary of solitude, you meet the purest version of yourself. Silence becomes the mirror reflecting your deepest truths, and in that stillness, you rise above the noise of the world. Isolation is not escape; it is the path to transcendence. It is in moments of solitude that you discover the clarity of your inner voice, separate from the distractions of external influences. When you are alone, you are forced to confront yourself—your fears, desires, and aspirations. This confrontation is where true growth begins.

> Solitude offers a rare opportunity to reconnect with your deeper purpose, allowing you to refine your thoughts and intentions. While others may seek validation from the outside world, you find strength in your own presence. It is through isolation that you cultivate wisdom, understanding, and resilience. In this space, you build the inner foundation necessary to rise above life's challenges. True elevation does not come from external praise or success, but from mastering the art of being alone with yourself and growing into the highest version of who you are meant to be.

* * *

"Life will discipline those who cannot discipline themselves."

The universe is a gentle teacher but a relentless corrector. Without self-discipline, life imposes its own lessons, often with greater force than we would choose. Mastery of self is the first step toward mastering life. Self-discipline is the foundation upon which all success and personal growth are built. Without it, we drift aimlessly, reacting to circumstances rather than shaping them.

When we lack discipline, the world tends to correct us in harsh ways, forcing us to learn through struggle and discomfort. Life, in its wisdom, provides opportunities for growth, but without the strength of self-control, we may miss those opportunities or waste them in impulsive decisions. Discipline, however, is not about rigid control, but about choosing the right actions at the right time, consistently.

True freedom comes from the ability to choose our path with intention, and this only comes through the practice of discipline. It is the key to overcoming distractions, remaining focused on long-term goals, and achieving inner peace. Once we master our own habits, desires, and impulses, we are able to face life with confidence, direction, and resilience. The discipline we cultivate within ourselves is what ultimately shapes the life we live and determines how we navigate its challenges.

* * *

"Self-mastery is the foundation of spiritual strength."

To command the outer world, you must first reign over your inner realm. Self-awareness, discipline, and inner peace are the pillars of true power. In mastering yourself, you unlock the door to infinite potential. True strength is not about controlling others or conquering external challenges; it is about having the discipline to control your own mind, emotions, and actions. It is the internal mastery of your thoughts, reactions, and desires that creates the foundation for a life of purpose and fulfillment. Self-awareness is the first step toward self-mastery. By understanding your thoughts, emotions, and behaviors, you gain the power to change them. Self-discipline follows, helping you stay committed to your goals even in the face of adversity. When you achieve inner peace, you are no longer swayed by external circumstances or the opinions of others. You become steadfast in your purpose, unaffected by distractions, and in full command of your mind.

> Self-mastery is the process of continuously growing and refining yourself, overcoming limiting beliefs, and aligning your actions with your deepest values. It is through this journey that you discover your true strength, unlocking the potential to achieve greatness and live a life that is fully aligned with your higher purpose.

* * *

"Every battle is won in the mind first."

Victory is not born on the battlefield but in the quiet corners of your thoughts. Conquer doubt, fear, and distraction, and the external world will bend to your will. The mind is the architect of destiny. Before any physical action can manifest, it first begins in the mind. It is through our thoughts that we create our perceptions, our beliefs, and ultimately, our reality. A disciplined mind can turn obstacles into opportunities, transforming adversity into strength.

The battles we face are not always seen on the outside. Often, they are fought in the silence of our own thoughts, where doubt creeps in and fear attempts to paralyze us. It is in these moments that we must learn to master our mind. When we control our thoughts, we control the outcome of our actions. The mind is powerful, and when it is aligned with purpose, it becomes an unstoppable force.

> Every challenge in life is an invitation to overcome the limiting beliefs we hold within ourselves. Once we conquer the internal battle of fear and doubt, we gain the courage and clarity to tackle the external world. Victory, then, is not just a result of physical strength or skill, but of the mental fortitude to persist in the face of adversity. The mind, when trained and focused, is capable of achieving greatness beyond imagination.

* * *

"Master your thoughts, and you master your life."

Your thoughts are the seeds of your reality. Tend to them with care, for they grow into the garden of your existence. Control your mind, and you control the world you create. The mind is a fertile ground where every belief, idea, and emotion takes root and grows. What you plant in your thoughts will eventually blossom into the experiences you encounter. If you nurture positive, empowering thoughts, you will harvest a life filled with success, peace, and fulfillment. However, if your mind is consumed with negativity, fear, and doubt, it will only bear the fruits of struggle and limitation.

To master your life, you must first master your thoughts. This requires constant awareness and discipline. It means taking responsibility for the thoughts you allow to take root in your mind and weeding out those that no longer serve you. Every thought has the power to shape your emotions, which in turn influence your actions and decisions. By consciously choosing empowering thoughts, you take control of your emotions and the outcomes they lead to.

> Your mind is the creator of your reality. When you control your thoughts, you unlock the ability to shape your experiences and craft the life you desire. Mastering your thoughts is not a one-time achievement, but an ongoing practice of staying focused, being mindful, and nurturing a mindset that serves your highest good. As you do this, you will begin to notice how your life begins to align with the positive vision you've cultivated in your mind.

* * *

"Your mind is your most valuable asset."
The mind is the gateway to all possibility, the wellspring of creativity and power. Guard it fiercely, nurture it wisely, and it will unlock doors you never knew existed. It is through the mind that we perceive the world and create our reality. Every idea, action, and innovation begins as a thought, making the mind the ultimate creator of all we experience. The quality of your thoughts determines the quality of your life, and thus, protecting and enhancing the mind becomes essential for personal growth and success.

Like any valuable asset, your mind requires care, attention, and protection. If you allow negative thoughts, distractions, and toxic influences to enter, they can weaken its power. However, when you nourish your mind with knowledge, positivity, and clarity, it becomes a powerful force capable of transforming your world. To unlock the full potential of your mind, you must constantly invest in its development — through learning, reflection, and mindfulness.

A well-maintained mind is a fountain of limitless possibilities, able to innovate, solve problems, and dream beyond the confines of what seems possible. Your thoughts shape your actions, your actions shape your habits, and your habits ultimately determine the course of your life. By recognizing the immense power within your mind, you give yourself the opportunity to tap into an infinite source of strength, creativity, and success.

* * *

"Protect your thoughts as you would your most prized possession."

Thoughts are the architects of your reality, the silent builders of your world. Shield them from negativity, and you will craft a life of beauty and abundance. The mind is constantly creating, even when we are unaware of it. Each thought that enters our mind is like a seed, planted into the soil of our subconscious. Whether positive or negative, these seeds grow and shape the life we experience. Therefore, protecting your thoughts is crucial to ensuring that only the most empowering, life-affirming beliefs take root.

In a world full of distractions, negativity, and outside influences, it's easy for our thoughts to become clouded. But when you guard your mind with awareness and intention, you create a powerful force for good in your life. Like a precious possession, your thoughts should be treated with reverence. Be mindful of the thoughts you allow to occupy your mind, as they will shape your emotions, actions, and ultimately, your reality.

> A disciplined mind is not one that is free of negative thoughts, but one that recognizes them and chooses not to engage with them. It is the practice of redirecting your mind toward positivity, clarity, and focus, ensuring that negativity does not take root. The more you protect your thoughts from destructive influences, the more you cultivate a life of peace, success, and joy. What you think is what you become, and by guarding your thoughts, you protect the very foundation of your future.

* * *

"A calm mind is a focused mind."

In the stillness of a tranquil mind, clarity emerges like the dawn. A calm mind sees clearly, acts decisively, and moves through life with purpose and grace. When the mind is calm, it is free from the noise of distractions, anxieties, and external pressures. It is in this state of serenity that true focus can be cultivated. A calm mind does not scatter its energy but directs it with precision toward the tasks at hand.

Without calmness, the mind becomes cluttered, making it difficult to make clear decisions or take meaningful action. But when the mind is still, it becomes like a clear mirror, reflecting the truth of the situation without distortion. In this clarity, you find the strength to move forward with purpose and confidence, unshaken by the chaos around you.

> A focused mind brings with it a deep sense of empowerment. It is no longer at the mercy of fleeting thoughts or emotions but is instead guided by intention. With calmness comes the ability to prioritize, to act with purpose, and to move steadily toward your goals. The calm mind allows for better problem-solving, greater creativity, and the ability to remain composed under pressure. By cultivating peace within, you open the door to focused action and a life that flows with grace.

* * *

"Peace of mind leads to clarity and direction."

When the storm within subsides, the path ahead becomes clear. Inner peace is the compass that guides you through life's chaos, illuminating the way forward. In a world filled with constant noise, distractions, and uncertainties, peace of mind is a rare but invaluable treasure. When the mind is calm and at peace, it is no longer clouded by confusion, fear, or doubt. Instead, it becomes sharp, clear, and focused.

Peace of mind allows you to see the world as it truly is, not distorted by stress or emotional turbulence. It brings clarity to your decisions, helping you to choose your direction with confidence. Without peace, the path ahead can appear overwhelming or unclear. But with inner tranquility, you can navigate through even the most difficult challenges with a clear sense of purpose.

> Peace also brings a sense of balance, allowing you to respond to life's uncertainties with grace and wisdom. It is not the absence of problems, but the ability to remain steady and centered despite them. When you cultivate peace within, you find direction in your life, as your thoughts and actions align with your true purpose. Inner peace leads to mental clarity, and mental clarity leads to the ability to make decisions that are in harmony with your highest self.

Chapter 2: Embracing Growth and Transformation

"Forgive yourself and move forward."
Self-forgiveness is the act of releasing the chains of the past. It is the first step toward healing, the moment you choose to honor your growth over your mistakes. In letting go, you create space for new beginnings. To forgive yourself is not to forget or excuse past actions but to acknowledge that you are human, and growth comes from learning, not perfection. Holding onto guilt or regret only binds you to past experiences, preventing you from fully embracing the potential of the present and the future.
Self-forgiveness allows you to shed the weight of your past mistakes, offering you the freedom to step into your highest self. By choosing to forgive, you acknowledge that you did the best you could with the knowledge and circumstances available at that time. Each moment is an opportunity to learn, grow, and evolve. To forgive yourself is to release the emotional burden and to accept that you are not defined by your mistakes but by your willingness to grow and improve.

In letting go of self-blame, you open the door to self-compassion and inner peace. It is a transformative act of kindness toward yourself, one that allows you to move forward with greater clarity, courage, and strength. With forgiveness comes the liberation to pursue new goals, embrace new opportunities, and create a life that aligns with your true potential. Self-forgiveness is the key to personal transformation, and it is the foundation for a future filled with possibility.

* * *

"Holding onto guilt and regret hinders your spiritual growth."

Guilt and regret are anchors, tethering you to moments that no longer exist. They trap you in the past, preventing you from fully embracing the present and future. These emotions act as weights, keeping your spirit grounded when it longs to rise. When you hold on to guilt, you are not only reliving past mistakes but also closing the door to forgiveness and healing. Regret, too, keeps you stuck in a cycle of 'what could have been' instead of empowering you to create 'what will be.'

Letting go of guilt and regret is an essential step toward spiritual freedom. It is the release of past burdens that allows your soul to breathe and expand. True spiritual growth begins when you stop judging yourself and start accepting yourself as you are. This does not mean ignoring your past mistakes but rather understanding that they were part of your journey, shaping you into the person you are today. Every experience, whether joyful or painful, holds wisdom if you are open to learning from it.

Releasing guilt and regret allows you to cultivate a sense of peace within, and from that peace comes the clarity to move forward with intention and purpose. Growth begins where self-judgment ends. Once you stop holding yourself captive to the past, you make room for self-compassion, inner peace, and spiritual development. Your journey becomes one of empowerment, where every step is taken with the full knowledge that you are not defined by your past but by the choices you make today.

* * *

"The harder the path, the higher the elevation."
The steepest climbs lead to the most breathtaking views. Life's challenges, though daunting, are often the very experiences that shape us into stronger, more resilient individuals. The road to personal growth and success is rarely smooth or easy, but it is in these struggles that we find our true potential. Every obstacle faced, every setback endured, becomes a stepping stone toward greater heights. The difficulty of the journey is directly proportional to the beauty of the rewards that await at the summit.

Embrace the struggle, for it is the forge in which your strength is tempered and your spirit refined. It is through adversity that we discover what we are truly capable of. Just as gold is purified in fire, so too is your character strengthened through hardship. Each challenge presents an opportunity to learn, to evolve, and to rise above the limitations you once thought were insurmountable.

The higher the mountain, the more breathtaking the view. The path may be long, the climb may be difficult, but the moment you reach the top, you will see the world in a way that only those who have persevered can. It is in overcoming life's greatest challenges that you find a deeper sense of fulfillment, knowing that you had the courage to walk the hardest path and emerge victorious.

* * *

"Growth and success are often born through hardship and perseverance."
Adversity is the soil in which greatness grows. Like a seed planted in rocky soil, success is often nurtured through hardship. The struggles you face in life are not obstacles to your progress; they are opportunities for growth. Each challenge presents a lesson that sharpens your character and strengthens your resolve. It is through adversity that you cultivate the qualities necessary for success: resilience, patience, and determination.
Each challenge is a seed of opportunity, and perseverance is the water that brings it to life. Without perseverance, these seeds would remain dormant. It is the relentless pursuit of your goals, even when the road is tough, that ensures your dreams take root and flourish. Success doesn't arrive overnight, but through sustained effort, it grows over time, nourished by your commitment to keep moving forward.

Without struggle, there is no strength. The weight you lift today is what builds the muscles of tomorrow. It is in the darkest times that your inner strength is forged. Through perseverance, you transform challenges into triumphs. Growth, therefore, is not just a result of smooth, effortless progress; it is the outcome of overcoming obstacles, staying steadfast, and continuing to strive even when the path is unclear. The success that emerges from this perseverance is not only sweeter but more deeply appreciated because it is earned, not given.

* * *

"You are not defined by your past."
The past is a chapter, not the entire story. Every person carries the weight of experiences, mistakes, and victories, but those are not what define you. They are lessons, stepping stones on your journey, but they do not determine your worth or your future. The past is behind you, a finished chapter that holds no power over your ability to grow, change, or create a new narrative.
It is a teacher, not a jailer. Your past offers wisdom, but it does not imprison you. It is through the lessons learned from previous struggles and triumphs that you gain the clarity to move forward. The chains of regret or past mistakes only hold you if you allow them to. When you choose to let go of those limitations, you release the past's grip and open yourself to new possibilities.

Release its grip, and you step into the infinite possibilities of the present moment. The future is a blank canvas, waiting for you to paint your masterpiece. Every new day offers fresh opportunities to redefine who you are and what you can achieve. You are not bound by the limitations of yesterday. Your power lies in the present moment, where you have the freedom to create the future you desire, unburdened by past labels.

* * *

"Let go of past mistakes to embrace your future."
Mistakes are not failures but lessons etched in the fabric of your journey. Each misstep, each challenge faced, holds invaluable wisdom that shapes who you are today. They are not marks of defeat but rather stepping stones that lead you toward greater understanding and resilience. The beauty of life lies not in perfection but in growth—every mistake is a building block in the foundation of your strength.

Release their weight, and you will rise lighter, freer, and ready to embrace the future. Holding on to past mistakes only burdens your soul and clouds your vision. By letting go, you free yourself from the shackles of regret and open the door to new opportunities. Embrace the lessons of the past, but do not allow them to define you. Your future is waiting, untainted by past mistakes, ready for you to step into it with clarity, confidence, and renewed energy.

* * *

"Embrace challenges as opportunities for growth."
Challenges are not obstacles but invitations to evolve. They are the universe's way of asking, "How much do you want to grow?" Every challenge presents a chance to step outside your comfort zone, to push beyond the limits you once thought were fixed. Rather than seeing them as barriers, view them as bridges—pathways that lead to greater strength, wisdom, and understanding.

> Embrace them with an open heart, for they are the very catalysts that fuel your transformation. Each challenge you face holds a hidden gift, a lesson waiting to be uncovered, and an opportunity to tap into your limitless potential. Through struggle comes strength, and through persistence comes progress. The greater the challenge, the more expansive your growth. When you learn to embrace challenges as part of your journey, you unlock the door to boundless possibilities.

* * *

"Adversity shapes the character of the soul."
The trials you endure are the chisel that sculpts your spirit. Just as a sculptor carefully chisels away at raw marble, adversity removes the unnecessary, revealing the strength and beauty hidden within. Each hardship serves as a defining moment, a test that builds your inner fortitude and deepens your understanding of life's purpose.

Through pain and struggle, you discover who you truly are—your capacity for resilience, your ability to rise above the challenges, and your determination to keep moving forward. Each challenge faced and overcome adds to the depth of your character, molding you into a person of strength, wisdom, and grace.

> Adversity is not something to be feared, but embraced as a transformative force. The struggles you encounter shape your soul in ways that comfort and ease never could. Every trial is a stroke of divine artistry, shaping you into a masterpiece of resilience and wisdom, ready to face the world with courage and conviction.

* * *

"Strength comes from overcoming what you thought you couldn't."
True strength is not simply about physical power or the ability to endure; it is forged in the moments when you face the seemingly impossible and find within yourself the courage to push forward. Strength is born in the quiet victories, the ones no one sees—the decision to keep going when you feel like giving up, to rise again after each fall, and to defy the limits you once believed were insurmountable.

Each challenge you face becomes a test of your resilience, and every victory, no matter how small, builds a foundation of strength that nothing can break. When you surpass the limits of your fears, doubts, and insecurities, you unlock your true potential.

The triumph of the human spirit is a powerful thing. It is the ability to rise above despair, to stand tall in the face of adversity, and to embrace the idea that the only true limitations are the ones you place on yourself. Through perseverance and faith in your own abilities, you discover that the things you once thought impossible are not only achievable but are the very moments where your strength is born.

* * *

"Every obstacle is a stepping stone to your greater self."
Obstacles are often perceived as barriers, but in truth, they are invitations to grow. Each challenge you face is a lesson in disguise, a moment to test your resolve, and an opportunity to break free from your limitations. The universe does not place roadblocks in your path to deter you; rather, it positions them to elevate you, to show you the strength and resilience that reside within.

Every obstacle holds the potential for transformation. When faced with a challenge, you are presented with a choice: to succumb to frustration or to embrace it as an opportunity to grow stronger, wiser, and more capable. With every step forward, no matter how difficult, you inch closer to your greater self—the person you are meant to become.

The road may not always be smooth, but the rough patches are where the most significant growth occurs. As you overcome each obstacle, you uncover hidden strengths, learn new lessons, and develop a deeper understanding of your own potential. Each stepping stone, no matter how large or small, is part of the journey that shapes you into the best version of yourself.

** * **

"Growth is uncomfortable but necessary."

Growth requires you to step out of your comfort zone, to venture into the unknown, where the familiar no longer guides you. It is in these moments of discomfort that the seeds of transformation are planted. The process of growth often feels like an uphill battle, where the challenges seem overwhelming and the path unclear. Yet, it is this very discomfort that fuels your evolution.

The discomfort you feel in the face of growth is not a sign of failure but a confirmation that you are moving in the right direction. It is through discomfort that you shed old beliefs, outdated patterns, and limiting habits. The process may be painful, but it is necessary. Like a seed pushing through the soil, growth is a struggle against resistance, but the result is worth it: the blossoming of your fullest potential.

As you move through this uncomfortable phase, remember that growth is the gateway to new opportunities, new strengths, and new horizons. It is only through discomfort that you break free from the confines of the past and step into a life that is limitless, abundant, and full of possibility.

* * *

"Change comes through action, not just intention."
Intention is the spark, the starting point of every transformation. However, without action, it remains just a dream. Intentions are like seeds planted in the soil of possibility, but it is the deliberate steps you take that nourish those seeds and make them grow. Change is not a passive process—it requires courage, effort, and persistence.

To bring your intentions to life, you must embrace the discomfort of action. You must step boldly into the unknown, trusting that each move you make, no matter how small, is a step closer to the life you desire. The journey from intention to reality is paved with consistent action, even when doubt or fear tries to hold you back.

Action is the bridge between where you are and where you want to be. It is the commitment to moving forward, even when the path isn't clear. Change is not a product of wishing or hoping but of doing and persevering.

Chapter 3: The Journey to Inner Peace

"Tune with the highest frequency within; this is where you will meet God."

The divine spark within you is not a distant concept but an inherent part of your being. This sacred frequency is the vibration of the soul, a harmonious resonance that connects you to the universe and the Creator. It is the highest state of being, where your thoughts, emotions, and actions align with the truth of your divine nature.

When you tune into this inner harmony, you elevate yourself beyond the noise and distractions of the external world. It is in this stillness, this sacred space, that you find the purest connection to God. It is not through outer rituals or external searches, but through the deep knowing and stillness within.

This frequency is ever-present, waiting for you to attune to it. As you quiet the mind and release the clatter of the world, you find the doorway to divine communion. It is here, in the center of your being, that you meet God—not as an abstract figure but as a living, breathing presence that guides, nurtures, and uplifts you.

By embracing this inner frequency, you awaken to your highest purpose, experiencing the divine flow that connects all things. It is the greatest peace, the truest form of love, and the most profound truth you will ever know.

* * *

"Connect with the divine by cultivating inner peace and harmony."

The divine is not distant, nor is it found in grand gestures or loud declarations. It resides within you, in the quiet spaces of your heart, where true peace and harmony live. To connect with the divine is to turn inward, seeking stillness in the midst of the chaos of the world.

Inner peace is the foundation upon which all spiritual connections are built. It is in this space of calm that you can hear the whispers of the universe, the gentle nudges that guide you toward your higher purpose. As you cultivate this peace, you align yourself with the flow of divine energy, creating a sanctuary within where love, clarity, and wisdom naturally emerge.

Harmony, too, is key in this connection. Just as an orchestra requires the perfect alignment of instruments to produce a beautiful symphony, your life requires the alignment of your thoughts, emotions, and actions to create harmony within. When you live in harmony with yourself, you are in tune with the universe, and the divine can flow effortlessly through you.

By nurturing inner peace and harmony, you create an open channel to the divine. It is here, in the stillness and alignment of your soul, that you experience the sacred presence that guides you, supports you, and uplifts you toward your greatest potential.

* * *

"Silence is a powerful teacher."
In the stillness, the mind clears, and the noise of the world fades away. Silence is not an absence but a presence—a sacred space where the soul can be heard. In a world constantly bombarded by information, distractions, and external expectations, silence becomes a sanctuary for true wisdom to emerge.

It is in the quiet moments that the deepest truths are revealed. When the mind is quiet, the heart speaks. The answers we search for are often not found in loud debates or hurried decisions but in the peace and calm that silence provides. Silence allows us to listen deeply—not just to the world around us, but to the whispers of our own spirit, guiding us toward clarity and understanding.

This powerful teacher does not impose, but invites. It is in this quiet that we reflect, process, and connect with our higher selves. Through silence, we begin to understand the vastness of our own inner world and the interconnectedness of all things. The wisdom imparted in silence is not always loud or immediate, but it is profound and lasting. It teaches us patience, presence, and the art of listening—to ourselves, to others, and to the divine.

In embracing silence, we open the door to a deeper connection with the truth that resides within us all.

* * *

"In stillness, clarity emerges."
In the quiet of stillness, the mind finds its natural state—calm and undistracted. It is here, in the absence of noise, that clarity finds its way to the surface. When we allow ourselves moments of peace, the fog of confusion begins to dissipate, revealing truths that were once hidden. Stillness allows us to see things clearly, without the distortion of stress, fear, or external influences.
In the rush of everyday life, it's easy to get lost in the chaos of thoughts, emotions, and obligations. But when we pause and create space for silence, the answers we've been seeking begin to emerge. Clarity is not a sudden revelation, but a quiet unfolding. It requires patience and presence—the ability to sit in the stillness and trust that the truth will come to us, in its own time.

> The mind, when allowed to rest, operates in its most powerful and clear state. In this space, intuition grows, and wisdom surfaces effortlessly. When we embrace stillness, we create the perfect environment for clarity to take root and grow. This peaceful silence is where true understanding blossoms, guiding us toward decisions that are aligned with our highest selves.

* * *

"Patience is a silent virtue."

Patience is not simply the act of waiting; it is a quiet, inner strength that allows us to trust in life's natural rhythm. It is the ability to endure without anxiety, to remain steadfast even when the world around us seems uncertain. Patience teaches us that there is wisdom in the waiting, that every moment holds purpose, even if it is not immediately clear.

In a world that values speed and instant gratification, patience stands as a quiet rebellion. It is the virtue that asks us to slow down and trust that everything is unfolding as it should. This silent virtue is not passive; it is active in its surrender to life's timing. The true power of patience lies in the acceptance that there is a season for everything, and all things come to fruition when they are meant to.

> When we practice patience, we free ourselves from the burden of worry. We no longer feel the need to rush, to force outcomes, or to seek control over the unfolding of events. Instead, we find peace in the understanding that all things have their time. Patience invites us to be present, to honor the journey, and to trust that everything is moving in its perfect timing.

* * *

"Let time and wisdom heal your soul."

Time, in its quiet, unhurried flow, is a master healer. It softens the sharpest pains, dulls the deepest sorrows, and gradually replaces the ache with the wisdom born of experience. While time works its magic, wisdom stands by, offering its guidance. It teaches us that every wound, no matter how deep, has the potential to become a wellspring of strength.

In the moments when we feel lost or broken, it is easy to forget that healing is a process, not an event. But with patience and faith, time reveals its gifts. It teaches us to see our struggles as lessons, each one shaping our character and fortifying our spirit. Wisdom, too, invites us to reflect on the value of those difficult moments, to understand how they have contributed to our growth.

> Together, time and wisdom guide us to a place of wholeness. They help us navigate our pain with grace, reminding us that healing is not about forgetting the past, but about integrating its lessons into the fabric of who we are. In time, the soul learns to let go of its burdens, and wisdom emerges, showing us the beauty in the scars we carry.

* * *

"Peace is a weapon; wear it always."
In a world constantly in motion, where distractions and disturbances are ever-present, peace becomes an invaluable asset. It is not a passive state but a powerful tool that shields you from the noise, the conflict, and the turmoil around you. Inner peace is like armor for the soul, a protective layer that ensures no external force can penetrate your center.

When you cultivate peace within, it becomes a weapon of resilience, an unshakable foundation from which you face life's challenges. No matter how chaotic the world becomes, peace allows you to remain grounded and steadfast, unaffected by the temporary storms that surround you.

This peace is not the absence of conflict but the ability to remain undisturbed despite it. It's the calm in the eye of the storm, the quiet strength that allows you to act from a place of clarity and centeredness. Wearing peace is a choice, a conscious decision to prioritize harmony over discord, tranquility over tension.

> In moments of chaos, remember that peace is your greatest defense. It's not just a state of mind; it's a way of being. The more you cultivate it, the stronger and more invulnerable you become. When you wear peace, you wear the armor of the soul, making you impervious to the forces that seek to disturb your balance.

* * *

"Inner peace is the ultimate form of resilience."
In a world filled with unpredictability and challenges, inner peace becomes your greatest asset. It is the bedrock upon which resilience is built. When your mind is at peace, it becomes unshakable, unbothered by external chaos or hardship.
This peace is not merely the absence of conflict, but the ability to remain centered and composed even in the face of adversity. Like a calm ocean, it does not allow the waves of life's difficulties to disturb its depths. Instead, it provides the clarity and strength to navigate through the storms of life with grace and unwavering stability.

True resilience is not defined by how many times you fall, but by your ability to rise, grounded in your inner peace. It is the quiet strength that empowers you to face any challenge, knowing that no external force can unsettle the foundation within. With inner peace, you have the unwavering center that allows you to endure hardships, bounce back stronger, and emerge from each trial not just unscathed, but more resilient and wise.

> Cultivating inner peace is the key to becoming truly resilient. It is the unmovable center that carries you through the ups and downs, making you invulnerable to the forces of negativity that often seek to weaken you. Through inner peace, you unlock the power to remain steady and strong, no matter what life throws your way.

* * *

"Peace begins within."

True peace is not a product of external circumstances, but rather a creation that originates from deep within you. The journey to peace begins in the quiet spaces of your heart, where you allow stillness and harmony to settle. It is in these moments of introspection and self-connection that peace begins to take root. When you cultivate inner harmony, it acts like a seed planted in fertile soil. As it grows, it begins to radiate outward, touching every aspect of your life. Just as light emanates from the core of the sun, your inner peace has the power to illuminate the world around you, creating an atmosphere of calm and tranquility wherever you go.

This peace is contagious; it spreads like a ripple in water, influencing those you encounter. The more you nurture your own inner peace, the more you create a peaceful environment, not just for yourself but for others as well. It becomes a powerful force, transforming not only your own heart but the hearts of those you meet.

> In a world often filled with noise, conflict, and uncertainty, the most profound change begins with the individual. By tending to your own peace, you set the foundation for a world of collective peace. Therefore, the journey starts with you—the more peace you create within, the more you will witness the peace that surrounds you.

* * *

"Inner peace is the foundation of peace in the world around you."
In a world that often feels chaotic and overwhelming, the key to true peace begins within you. When you find peace within your own heart, you become a living example of what it means to live in harmony with the world. Your inner peace becomes the cornerstone from which the peace around you is built.
As you cultivate this inner calm, it radiates outward like a beacon of light, shining through the turbulence of everyday life. Your presence becomes a source of tranquility for others, and through your actions, you inspire others to seek and create peace within themselves as well.

When you are centered in your own peace, you are no longer reactive to the external chaos around you. Instead, you are a steady anchor, unaffected by the storm. Your calm energy has the power to transform tense situations and create spaces of serenity, no matter how much unrest surrounds you.

> The ripples of your inner peace extend far beyond you, touching everyone and everything you encounter. In this way, your peace not only nurtures your soul but also plays a part in creating a more peaceful world for others. Remember, the world changes when each individual cultivates peace within themselves. You are the foundation of the peace you seek in the world.

* * *

"Focus on the present moment."
The present moment is the only real moment, the only space where life truly unfolds. The past is gone, and the future is yet to come, but the present is where everything happens. It is where you have the power to act, to experience, and to create. Focusing on the now allows you to embrace life in its purest form, unburdened by regrets or anxieties.

When you immerse yourself fully in the present, you connect with the essence of life itself. You become attuned to the beauty of the moment, whether it is in a conversation, a task, or simply breathing. The distractions of the past and future no longer have control over you. In this space, you find peace, for peace is born in the present.

Clarity also emerges when you focus on the here and now. Your mind quiets, and the noise of worry and expectation fades away. You begin to see things as they truly are, without distortion, and make decisions with a clear heart and mind.

> In a world that pulls you in many directions, focusing on the present moment is a powerful act of self-care and mindfulness. It is a reminder that life's beauty lies in the simple moments, and by being present, you unlock a sense of fulfillment that cannot be found in the past or future.

* * *

"The present is the only time that truly exists."
The past is but a shadow, a collection of memories fading with time. The future is a dream, a horizon that always seems just out of reach. But the present is the only true reality, the only moment in which life unfolds. It is where your power lies, where your choices shape your path, and where your experiences come to life.

When you live in the present, you embrace the fullness of existence. Every breath, every action, every thought becomes meaningful because it is happening right now. The present is a gift, a fleeting moment to be cherished, for it is the only time you can ever truly live.

Often, we get caught up in the past, replaying old stories, or we anxiously await the future, hoping for things to change. But neither can give us what the present offers: the ability to act, to be, to feel, and to experience life fully. By anchoring yourself in the present, you free yourself from the weight of regret and the burden of worry, allowing you to experience peace and gratitude.

> Remember, the present is all you have. It is the bridge between who you were and who you will become. It is the space where dreams are made real, where love is expressed, and where joy is found. Embrace it, for in the present, you hold the key to living a fulfilled life.

Chapter 4: The Art of Living Authentically

"Settle for nothing less than whom you would like to mirror." The people you choose to surround yourself with play a significant role in shaping the person you become. They are mirrors reflecting aspects of your own potential, your strengths, and your weaknesses. The individuals you admire and look up to are not just figures of success, but also embodiments of the traits, values, and qualities you aspire to develop in yourself.

When you set your sights on those who inspire greatness—whether through their wisdom, courage, compassion, or resilience—you begin to align yourself with those same qualities. It's about choosing mentors and role models who push you toward personal growth, individuals whose actions and mindset elevate you to new heights.

Settling for anything less than the people who challenge and inspire you means settling for mediocrity. You deserve to be surrounded by those who elevate your spirit, who mirror the person you want to become, and who lead by example. Through their influence, you begin to reflect the best version of yourself.

* * *

"Strive to embody the qualities you admire in others."

The qualities you admire in others—whether it's their kindness, resilience, creativity, or integrity—are often traits that already exist within you, waiting to be nurtured. When you recognize these traits in others, it's not just admiration; it's a call to awaken those very qualities within yourself. The universe works in such a way that the things we appreciate in others are often reflections of the highest version of who we could be.

To admire someone is to recognize a part of your own potential that you haven't yet fully expressed. By striving to embody the same traits that inspire you, you embark on a journey of self-growth and self-discovery. It's not about imitating others but about drawing inspiration from them to cultivate the best version of yourself. In doing so, you elevate your own life while also inspiring those around you.

As you embody these qualities, you become not just an admirer, but a living example of the values you hold dear. You become a beacon of inspiration for others, reflecting the power of transformation through the cultivation of positive traits. In turn, those who admire you will see their own potential mirrored back to them, continuing the cycle of growth and inspiration.

> Embrace the qualities that speak to your heart, for in striving to embody them, you create a life of authenticity, influence, and meaningful connection.

* * *

"Change your ways, never your principles."
In the journey of life, adaptability is one of the most powerful tools for personal growth. The world around us is ever-changing, and the ability to adjust to new circumstances, learn from experiences, and embrace innovation is crucial. However, while the methods and approaches we use to navigate life may evolve, our core values—the principles that define who we are—should remain steadfast.

Your principles are the foundation upon which your character is built. They are the compass that guides you through life's challenges, helping you to stay grounded no matter how much the landscape shifts. Integrity, honesty, kindness, and courage—these values are timeless, unchanging, and should never be compromised, no matter how the world around you changes.

Adapting your strategies, your behaviors, or your mindset to meet new situations is a sign of growth. It reflects your willingness to learn, change, and evolve with the times. But the essence of who you are—your moral compass—should always remain consistent. Stay true to your values, for they are the heart of your identity, the part of you that defines your purpose and drives you forward.

By changing your ways while preserving your principles, you allow yourself the freedom to grow without losing the core of who you are.

* * *

"Let your heart speak louder than your words."

The most powerful form of communication transcends the spoken word. It is the language of the heart—an unspoken connection that speaks louder than any sentence could. When your actions reflect the love, care, and compassion within you, the need for words diminishes. Your intentions, your sincerity, and your kindness all become visible through the way you interact with others, and this speaks volumes.

Too often, we rely on words to express ourselves, but words can be empty without the emotion behind them. True communication is not about the things you say, but about the feelings you convey and the energy you share. When your heart guides your actions, the message you send is crystal clear—authentic, heartfelt, and true.

In every moment, you have the power to communicate with your actions. A kind gesture, a listening ear, or a simple act of understanding can convey more than the most carefully crafted words ever could. When your heart is at the center of your interactions, you create deeper connections, foster trust, and cultivate a sense of peace that no amount of verbal communication can replicate.

> Let your heart lead, and your words will become secondary. Your presence will carry the message.

* * *

"Actions rooted in love resonate deeper than words."
Love is not just a sentiment expressed through words—it is a force that is felt through actions. While words can be fleeting, actions have the power to leave a lasting impression. When you act out of love, your intentions are clear, and the impact is profound. Love, when demonstrated through gestures, kindness, and compassion, transcends any verbal communication. It is felt in the warmth of a hug, the selflessness of a helping hand, and the quiet support that doesn't seek recognition.

When your actions align with love, they become a powerful language that speaks to the soul. They echo in the hearts of others, creating a bond that words alone cannot achieve. A kind word may uplift, but a loving action can heal, transform, and inspire.

> To live with love means to embody it in every moment, in every choice you make. It is not about what you say, but about what you do. Let your actions reflect the love within you, and you will leave an imprint on the world that is far more powerful than anything words could convey.

* * *

"The truth will set you free, but first it will make you uncomfortable."

Truth has a way of shaking us to our core. It often strips away the comforting layers of illusion and reveals what we have been avoiding or denying. Initially, the truth feels like a harsh force, a dissonance that disturbs our peace and challenges our beliefs. It may cause discomfort, resistance, and even pain, as we confront the reality of situations, actions, and choices we would rather ignore.

But in this discomfort lies the path to freedom. The truth, no matter how uncomfortable, holds the power to liberate us from the chains of falsehoods, self-deception, and denial. It is the key that unlocks our growth, our healing, and our transformation. The discomfort is temporary, but the freedom it brings is lasting.

By embracing the truth, we free ourselves from the weight of lies, guilt, and misunderstandings. It clears the fog in our minds and allows us to live more authentically, making choices that align with who we truly are. In the end, the discomfort gives way to a deeper sense of peace, clarity, and strength—an undeniable freedom that comes only through the courage to face the truth.

* * *

"Authenticity brings liberation."
To live authentically is to embrace your true self without the fear of judgment or the need to conform to societal expectations. It is a powerful act of self-liberation, one that frees you from the invisible chains of approval-seeking and external validation. When you stop measuring your worth by the standards of others and instead embrace your unique essence, you step into your full potential.

Authenticity is the path to personal freedom because it aligns your actions, thoughts, and feelings with your inner truth. It removes the weight of pretense and the pressure to fit into a mold that doesn't represent who you are. As you embrace your authenticity, you also let go of the fear of rejection and judgment, replacing them with a deep sense of peace and self-respect.

> True freedom is found in the absence of the need for external validation. When you are authentic, you no longer seek approval because you know your value doesn't depend on anyone's perception of you. In embracing who you are, you create space for growth, creativity, and true connection with others who appreciate you for the real you. Authenticity is the ultimate form of liberation—it frees you to live fully and unapologetically.

* * *

"Never chase, always attract."
In the pursuit of success and fulfillment, chasing after people, opportunities, or validation can often feel like running on a treadmill—constant motion without forward progress. The secret to true growth and success lies in attracting, not chasing. When you focus on becoming the best version of yourself—developing your skills, nurturing your values, and staying aligned with your purpose—you naturally magnetize the right people and opportunities.

Attraction is a subtle yet powerful force. It stems from inner confidence, authenticity, and the clarity of knowing who you are and what you want. When you stop desperately seeking approval or external validation, you release the energy of scarcity and instead embrace an abundance mindset. This shift allows you to draw people who resonate with your energy and opportunities that align with your purpose.

> By focusing on your personal growth and remaining grounded in your values, you create a magnetic force around you that attracts opportunities, relationships, and experiences that are meant to elevate you. Trust that the right things will come into your life when you stop chasing them. Instead, focus on being so aligned with your truth that they can't help but find their way to you.

* * *

"Focus on becoming the best version of yourself, and the right people will come."

When you focus on personal growth, you shift your energy and elevate your vibration. The world responds to the energy you put out. By becoming the best version of yourself—living authentically, nurturing your strengths, and embodying positivity—you create an aura that naturally attracts the right people, experiences, and opportunities.

People who resonate with your energy will be drawn to you. Authenticity has a magnetic quality; when you are true to yourself and confident in your path, others who share your values and vision will be drawn into your orbit. This isn't about seeking approval or approval-seeking behaviors; it's about being the fullest expression of who you are, without apology.

The right relationships—whether personal, professional, or spiritual—will naturally align with your energy. Focus on cultivating your own inner peace, growth, and authenticity, and the universe will bring the right people into your life at the right time.

* * *

"Live boldly, and unapologetically."
Fear often holds us back from living life to the fullest. But true freedom comes when you embrace your authenticity and let go of the need for approval. When you live boldly, you step into your power, unapologetically expressing who you are, without fear of judgment or rejection.

Living on your own terms means making choices that align with your deepest truths, even if they are unconventional or misunderstood. It's about embracing your uniqueness and daring to follow your own path, regardless of what others may think.

Remember, life is fleeting, and time wasted on fear or self-doubt is time you can never get back. Live fully, unapologetically, and with boldness, knowing that the world needs your unique light.

* * *

"True freedom is living life on your own terms."
Freedom is not just the absence of constraints; it is the ability to live authentically, making choices that reflect who you truly are. When you embrace your individuality, you no longer feel the need to conform to external expectations or societal norms. Instead, you act based on your inner truth and desires.

True freedom comes from within—it is the freedom to think, speak, and act according to your deepest values, without fear of judgment or rejection. It is about taking ownership of your life, your choices, and your destiny.

> When you claim your freedom, you break free from the shackles of other people's expectations and fully step into your own power. Living life on your own terms is the ultimate expression of self-love and authenticity.

Chapter 5: The Power of Belief and Intention

"Limited beliefs limit reality."

The beliefs you hold about yourself and the world around you form the lens through which you experience life. When you believe in your limitations, you unknowingly create barriers that restrict your potential. These self-imposed beliefs act as chains, keeping you from reaching your true capabilities.

To unlock a reality filled with infinite possibilities, you must first challenge and release those limiting beliefs. By embracing a mindset of abundance, growth, and possibility, you begin to see opportunities where you once saw obstacles.

> Your beliefs are not facts; they are perceptions. Shift your perspective, and you shift your reality. Break free from the constraints of limiting beliefs, and watch your world expand in ways you never thought possible.

* * *

"Focus on light till you become the light."

What you focus on expands, and the energy you radiate is influenced by where you direct your thoughts. When you focus on the light — positivity, kindness, love, and hope — these qualities begin to take root within you. As you cultivate this focus, you gradually become a beacon of light to those around you.

In a world often filled with darkness, the light you nurture within can illuminate the path for others, guiding them toward the same transformation. The more you embody the light, the more you become a reflection of it — not just for yourself, but for the world in need of hope and inspiration.

> Choose to focus on light, and you will become the very essence of it.

* * *

"Cultivate positivity, kindness, and compassion in your thoughts and actions."

The energy you put into the world comes back to you. By consciously nurturing positivity, kindness, and compassion, you create an environment where love and understanding can flourish. Your thoughts shape your reality, and when they are rooted in goodness, they spark a chain reaction of warmth and connection.

When your actions reflect these values, they send out ripples that touch those around you, encouraging them to pass on the same energy. The more you practice these qualities, the more you attract similar people and experiences into your life.

In a world that often feels fragmented, you can be the glue that binds hearts together through your actions and mindset. Let positivity be your guide, kindness your language, and compassion your way of living.

* * *

"Happiness is a choice, not a result."
Happiness does not depend on external circumstances or achievements; it is a mindset you can cultivate each day. It is the conscious decision to focus on the positive, to embrace gratitude, and to seek joy in the simple things.
No matter what life presents, you have the power to choose how you respond. By training your mind to see the beauty, the opportunity, and the blessings in every situation, you create a life filled with happiness.
Remember, the pursuit of happiness is not a distant goal but a practice that begins in the present moment. Choose to be happy, and happiness will follow you wherever you go.

* * *

"You hold the power to shape your happiness."
Happiness is not something that happens to you; it is something you actively create. By choosing to focus on the good, by practicing gratitude, and by shifting your mindset, you have the power to shape a life filled with joy and fulfillment.
Each day is an opportunity to take charge of your emotions and actions, to align your thoughts with positivity, and to let go of what doesn't serve your well-being. The key is within you — your outlook, your attitude, and your choices.

Remember, the power to cultivate happiness lies in your hands. Embrace it, and watch your world transform.

* * *

"Trust the universe; it has a plan for you."
The universe operates on a grander scale than we can always perceive. Even in moments of uncertainty, trust that everything is unfolding in your favor. Every experience, every challenge, and every twist in the road is part of a bigger plan that is leading you exactly where you need to be.

When the path ahead seems unclear, have faith in the unseen forces at work. Trust that the universe is guiding you toward growth, opportunity, and the fulfillment of your purpose. You are exactly where you need to be in this moment.

Embrace the journey, knowing that the universe has a plan for you.

* * *

"The universe always works in your favor if you align with it."
The universe is constantly in motion, offering opportunities and experiences for growth. When you align your actions, thoughts, and intentions with its natural flow, you step into harmony with its rhythm. In this alignment, you become a co-creator of your own destiny, where synchronicities appear, and doors open effortlessly.

Trust that by staying true to your purpose and remaining open to what comes your way, the universe will support your journey. It's not about forcing outcomes, but about embracing the flow and trusting the process. When you align with the universe, you will not only thrive—you will flourish beyond what you imagined possible.

* * *

"You are the creator of your reality."
Every thought you have, every belief you hold, and every action you take forms the foundation of the world around you. The reality you experience is a direct reflection of your inner world. When you take responsibility for your life, you empower yourself to design the path you wish to walk.

The power to transform your reality lies within you. By consciously choosing positive thoughts, aligning with your values, and taking purposeful action, you step into the role of the architect of your own destiny. You have the ability to create a life filled with meaning, fulfillment, and purpose.

* * *

"Your choices and beliefs shape the world you live in."
The world you experience is a reflection of the choices you make and the beliefs you hold. Every decision, no matter how small, ripples out and shapes the reality you live in. When you align your choices with positivity, gratitude, and your highest aspirations, you begin to craft a life filled with abundance, joy, and fulfillment.

Your beliefs act as the lens through which you see the world. If you believe in your potential and in the goodness of life, you will attract opportunities that reflect those truths. Choose wisely, and create a reality that supports your dreams and aspirations.

* * *

"You are worthy of all the good things life has to offer."
Embrace your inherent worthiness, for it is the key to unlocking the abundance that awaits you. When you truly believe that you deserve all the goodness life has to offer, you align yourself with the flow of blessings. Trust in your worth, and watch as opportunities, love, and success come into your life naturally. You are deserving of happiness, peace, and everything that nourishes your soul.

* * *

"Believe in your worthiness to receive abundance."
Abundance flows to those who recognize their own worthiness. It is your birthright to live a life full of blessings, prosperity, and joy. When you trust in your value, you open the doors for life to deliver everything you need. Embrace the truth that you deserve the best, and the universe will respond by bringing abundance into your life.

Chapter 6: The Path to Purpose and Fulfillment

"Mastery is a lifelong journey."
True mastery is not defined by a single achievement but by the ongoing pursuit of growth and knowledge. It's a path of continuous improvement, where each step brings you closer to your fullest potential. Embrace the journey with patience and passion, and you will find fulfillment in the progress, not just the destination.

* * *

"Consistent effort brings mastery in any field."
Success is not an overnight achievement, but the result of daily, consistent actions. It's the small, seemingly insignificant efforts that accumulate over time, building momentum and laying the foundation for greatness. The key is persistence. By continuing to show up day after day, even when results seem minimal, you are laying the groundwork for mastery. Trust the process, and remember, every small step brings you closer to achieving your ultimate goal.

* * *

"Life's greatest lessons come from the most unexpected places."

Wisdom has a way of finding us when we least expect it. Often, the most valuable lessons come during times of struggle, in moments of uncertainty, or from people and experiences we might have otherwise overlooked. Life's surprises are filled with opportunities for growth, and embracing them can lead to the most profound transformations. Stay open to the unexpected, for it is in these moments that true wisdom is born.

* * *

"Embrace every moment as a learning opportunity."
Life presents us with endless opportunities to learn and grow. Every experience, no matter how challenging or joyful, offers valuable insights that shape us. When we approach each moment with curiosity and openness, we unlock the potential for growth. Even mistakes and setbacks hold hidden lessons that can guide us toward a wiser, more fulfilled version of ourselves. So, embrace every moment, for it is through these experiences that we become the people we are meant to be.

* * *

"Understand the value of your time."

Time is the most valuable resource we possess, yet it is often the one we take for granted. Once a moment passes, it is gone forever, making it irreplaceable. Every second spent on unimportant tasks, distractions, or procrastination is a second you cannot reclaim. By recognizing the true value of your time, you begin to prioritize what matters most—whether it's personal growth, meaningful relationships, or achieving your goals. When you treat time as a precious commodity, you make conscious choices that lead to a more fulfilling and productive life.

* * *

* * *

"Time is the one resource you can never get back."
Time is the silent architect of your life. Every minute that passes is a moment you cannot reclaim. Unlike money, you cannot earn time back, and once it's gone, it leaves no trace. This makes time the most precious resource you have. The way you invest it shapes your future, your relationships, and your sense of purpose. By choosing to invest your time in meaningful pursuits—whether it's nurturing relationships, pursuing passions, or personal growth—you create a life full of richness and fulfillment. Every moment you waste is a lost opportunity, so make every second count toward building the life you truly desire.

* * *

"Live with purpose."
Living with purpose gives direction to your life. It's the compass that guides your decisions, motivates you through challenges, and fills your days with meaning. A life without purpose can feel aimless, but when you align yourself with your passions and core values, every action becomes intentional. Purpose brings

clarity and focus, helping you prioritize what truly matters. By living with purpose, you not only find fulfillment but also inspire others to pursue their own paths with conviction. Whether it's a career, a cause, or personal growth, let your purpose be the driving force that shapes your journey.

* * *

"Find meaning and passion in everything you do."

Every task, no matter how small, holds the potential for significance when approached with the right mindset. By infusing your actions with meaning, you transform the ordinary into something extraordinary. Passion is the fuel that turns routine into a rewarding experience. When you live with intention, you begin to see purpose in everything, from work to daily chores, from interactions with others to moments of solitude. It's not about what you do but how you do it. When you find passion in the process, joy naturally follows. Cultivate this mindset, and you will experience a richer, more fulfilling life.

* * *

* * *

"Every step you take brings you closer to your goals."

Success is built on the foundation of consistent, incremental progress. Every small action, no matter how insignificant it may seem at the time, is a step forward. It's easy to get overwhelmed by the big picture, but remembering that each step brings you closer helps maintain focus and motivation. Celebrate the small victories—each one is a reminder that you're moving in the right direction. Over time, these small steps add up to significant achievements, and before you know it, you've reached your goal. The journey is just as important as the destination, so embrace each moment and keep moving forward.

* * *

"Progress is a series of small steps forward."

> Success doesn't happen overnight, and it's rarely the result of a single large leap. Instead, it's the culmination of consistent, small steps that compound over time. Every action, every decision you make to keep moving forward, no matter how small, contributes to your progress. Don't get discouraged by the distance between where you are and where you want to be. Instead, focus on the next small step, trusting that it will bring you closer to your ultimate destination. Keep putting in the effort, and over time, you will see the results of your persistence and dedication.

* * *

"You are the sum of your habits."

The life you lead is the result of the choices you make every day, and those choices are shaped by your habits. Whether big or small, habits define your routine and, ultimately, your future. Positive habits, like daily exercise, mindful reflection, or consistent learning, will compound over time to create a life of success, growth, and fulfillment. On the other hand, negative habits can hold you back from reaching your full potential. The good news is, you have the power to change your habits and, in turn, transform your life. Start with small adjustments, build consistency, and watch as your habits begin to shape the life you desire.

* * *

"Your daily habits shape your life."
The small actions you take each day, often unnoticed, are the building blocks of your future. Whether it's dedicating time to personal growth, maintaining a positive mindset, or staying disciplined in your work, these daily habits compound over time. Success doesn't happen overnight; it is a result of consistently showing up and making small improvements day after day. Focus on cultivating habits that align with your values and goals, and you'll create a life that reflects your efforts. Every habit, no matter how small, contributes to the transformation of your life.

* * *

"Don't wait for opportunities; create them."

Opportunities are not passive gifts; they are the fruits of your actions, mindset, and effort. When you take initiative and step out of your comfort zone, you begin to shape your own destiny. Don't sit back and hope for the perfect moment. Instead, make the moment perfect by taking action. Whether it's starting a new project, networking with the right people, or learning new skills, you create your opportunities through your persistence and determination. Every step you take towards your goal is an opportunity in the making. Keep moving forward, and doors will open where there once were none.

* * *

"Opportunity is created through persistence and action."

Success doesn't just happen; it's the product of consistent effort and the courage to keep going, even when the path is unclear. Every step you take, every challenge you face, and every action you take brings you closer to your goal. The more persistent you are, the more doors open, often in unexpected ways. It's in the moments when you feel like giving up that true opportunities are born. Keep showing up, keep pushing forward, and you'll find that the world begins to open up to you. The only thing standing between you and opportunity is the will to take action.

Chapter 7: Courage and Resilience

"Find strength in your weaknesses."
What you perceive as weaknesses may hold the key to your greatest potential. Often, the struggles we face reveal deeper layers of strength and resilience that we didn't know existed. Embracing these vulnerabilities allows you to transform them into sources of power. When you stop fighting your weaknesses and start learning from them, you unlock a strength that is rooted in authenticity and self-awareness. Your challenges are the soil in which your most remarkable growth is nurtured. Embrace them, and you will find strength in places you least expect.

* * *

"What you perceive as your flaws may be your hidden strengths."
Often, the qualities we view as flaws are the very traits that set us apart and give us power. Embrace your uniqueness, for what makes you different is what allows you to shine. Your so-called flaws are not limitations but rather opportunities for growth and distinction. When you accept these aspects of yourself, you begin to realize they are the foundation of your strength. What you once saw as imperfections can become your greatest assets, empowering you to navigate life with confidence and authenticity.

* * *

"Let go of fear; embrace courage."

Fear often keeps us stuck in place, convincing us that we are incapable or unworthy. But fear is just an illusion, a barrier that only exists in our minds. Courage is not the absence of fear, but the willingness to act in spite of it. When you embrace courage, you choose to face the unknown, trusting that growth and strength lie on the other side of your fears. Let go of the hold fear has on you, and step boldly into the possibilities that await. The more you confront fear with courage, the more powerful you become.

* * *

"Courage is the absence of fear, not the absence of struggle." Courage doesn't mean living without fear—it means embracing fear and choosing to move forward anyway. It's not about avoiding the struggle but recognizing that the struggle is where you find your power. In the face of adversity, courage shows up as the willingness to continue despite challenges. Every obstacle you overcome is a testament to your inner strength. Embrace the struggle, for it is the foundation upon which true courage is built.

* * *

"Keep pushing forward, even when it's hard."

The road to success is rarely smooth. It is paved with challenges and obstacles that can make the journey feel overwhelming. But perseverance is what turns struggle into victory. Every step you take, even when it feels hard, is progress. Trust that each challenge you overcome is strengthening your resilience and getting you closer to your goals. When the journey feels tough, remember that the only way to fail is to stop moving forward. Keep going—your destination is worth it.

* * *

"Perseverance leads to success."
Success is a marathon, not a sprint. It is the result of consistent effort, determination, and the willingness to keep going despite setbacks. The path may be long, and the challenges may seem insurmountable at times, but the key to reaching your goals lies in your ability to persevere. Every small step forward counts, and with each moment of persistence, you are one step closer to your desired outcome. Keep moving, even when the progress feels slow—the finish line is ahead, and your perseverance will carry you there.

* * *

* * *

"Embrace the unknown with confidence."

The unknown is a vast expanse filled with endless possibilities. It is natural to feel fear or uncertainty when faced with unfamiliar territory, but it is precisely in these moments that growth occurs. By stepping into the unknown with confidence, you open yourself up to new opportunities and experiences. Embrace it as an adventure, a chance to learn, explore, and expand your limits. Trust in your ability to navigate the unknown, and you will find that it is often the key to unlocking your greatest potential.

* * *

"Great things await those who step into the unknown."
The unknown is where all possibilities begin. It may seem daunting at first, but beyond the comfort of what you know lies the potential for profound transformation. Stepping into unfamiliar territory is where growth happens, where challenges become stepping stones, and where the most fulfilling experiences are born. The rewards are often greater than what we can imagine, but only if we dare to take that first step. Embrace the unknown with courage, and you will uncover greatness you never knew existed.

Chapter 8: Love, Relationships, and Connection

"Elevate your circle to elevate your life."

The people you spend your time with have a profound impact on your mindset, energy, and growth. Surround yourself with individuals who challenge you, encourage your dreams, and support your ambitions. When you choose to be around those who inspire and uplift, you are more likely to rise to your fullest potential. Your environment plays a crucial role in your success, so curate a circle that pushes you toward becoming the best version of yourself.

* * *

* * *

"The people around you shape the trajectory of your life."

The relationships you nurture have the power to influence your path. When you surround yourself with individuals who uplift and challenge you, your life takes on a new direction, filled with growth and purpose. Choose to build connections with those who share your values, inspire your dreams, and support your ambitions. They not only mirror your potential but also amplify it, guiding you toward a future aligned with your true self.

* * *

"Your vibe attracts your tribe."
The energy you project into the world is magnetic. When you cultivate a mindset of positivity, authenticity, and kindness, you naturally attract people who resonate with those qualities. Your tribe will be a reflection of the energy you embody, so choose to be a source of light, and you will find yourself surrounded by individuals who share your values and vision, creating a community of mutual growth and support.

* * *

"Surround yourself with people who resonate with your energy."

The company you keep plays a crucial role in shaping your experiences. Surround yourself with individuals who share your values, uplift your spirit, and support your growth. These are the people who will empower you to reach new heights, challenge you to become your best self, and help you navigate life's challenges. A tribe of like-minded souls creates a harmonious environment where everyone can thrive together, fostering an atmosphere of mutual respect and growth.

* * *

* * *

"Love yourself first."
Self-love is the cornerstone of healthy relationships and personal happiness. When you cultivate love and compassion for yourself, you build the strength to offer love to others without fear or hesitation. By prioritizing your well-being and valuing your own worth, you create an inner peace that radiates outward, allowing you to give and receive love in its purest form. Only when you truly love yourself can you fully embrace and nurture the connections that bring joy and fulfillment into your life.

* * *

* * *

"Self-love is the foundation for loving others."

True love starts within. When you nurture and care for yourself, you create a space where love can flourish and grow. Just as you cannot pour from an empty cup, you cannot give love effectively if you are not first filled with it. By prioritizing your own well-being and embracing self-compassion, you build a foundation of love that expands outward. This not only enhances your relationships with others but also allows you to share your love in a way that is genuine, abundant, and uplifting.

Chapter 9: The Beauty of Simplicity and Gratitude

"The most beautiful things are often the most simple."

Simplicity holds a quiet, profound beauty. In our fast-paced world, it's easy to overlook the simple joys around us. Yet, it is often the small, unadorned moments—like a quiet walk, a warm smile, or the stillness of nature—that bring the deepest fulfillment. When you allow yourself to appreciate the simplicity of life, you open the door to a deeper sense of contentment. Beauty doesn't always need to be grand or complicated; it resides in the small, everyday experiences that remind us of the richness of existence.

* * *

* * *

"Find beauty in simplicity."

In a world that often celebrates excess and complexity, simplicity stands as a quiet testament to true beauty. When we strip away the clutter, whether in our surroundings or our lives, we reveal a clarity that allows us to truly appreciate what matters. Simplicity isn't about lack; it's about purity and intention. By focusing on the essentials, we free ourselves from distractions and allow the true essence of beauty to shine through. It is in the uncomplicated moments where we often find the deepest meaning and peace.

* * *

* * *

"Take responsibility for your own happiness."

Happiness is not something that can be given to you by others; it is something that comes from within. When you take ownership of your own joy, you stop relying on external circumstances or people to define your happiness. You begin to realize that your thoughts, choices, and actions play a crucial role in shaping your emotional state. By choosing positivity, gratitude, and self-love, you create an internal environment where happiness thrives. Remember, you hold the key to your own well-being, and the power to create joy lies in your hands.v

* * *

* * *

"Happiness begins with you, not external circumstances."

True happiness is not dependent on external factors but on your inner state of being. Cultivate joy within, and it will radiate outward. Happiness starts from within. When you find peace and joy inside yourself, nothing can take that away. Cultivate inner happiness by focusing on gratitude, self-acceptance, and letting go of negative influences. As you develop your inner world, your outer world will reflect this transformation, bringing positive energy and fulfillment into every part of your life.

* * *

"Freedom begins with the mind."
True freedom is the liberation of the mind from fear and limitation. Free your thoughts, and you will free your life. Often, the greatest obstacles to our freedom are the beliefs and fears that we carry in our minds. When we release these mental barriers, we open ourselves to endless possibilities. Freedom is not just about external circumstances; it is a state of mind. The moment you shift your thoughts from limitation to possibility, you begin to live a life of true freedom.

* * *

"True freedom is found when you release mental and emotional chains."

Let go of the beliefs and emotions that bind you, and you will experience the true essence of freedom. Many of the limitations we face are not imposed by the outside world but by the thoughts we nurture and the emotions we carry. Fear, guilt, regret, and self-doubt can quietly shape our lives if left unexamined. By confronting these inner barriers and choosing to release them, we create space for clarity, peace, and liberation. True freedom is not about escape—it's about inner peace and self-acceptance.

Chapter 10: Creating Your Reality

"Life is not about waiting; it's about creating."
Don't wait for the perfect moment; create it. Take action, and you will shape the life you desire. The illusion of a "right time" often keeps us stuck in hesitation, waiting for ideal conditions that may never come. But life rewards those who take initiative, who build their dreams with intention and courage. Every moment holds the potential for growth and transformation—if you choose to act. You are the artist of your life; pick up the brush and paint the reality you envision.

* * *

"Take initiative and craft the life you want."
Your life is a blank canvas, and you are the artist. Take bold strokes, and you will create a masterpiece. Every action you take is a brushstroke on the painting of your destiny. Waiting for change keeps you in place, but creating it empowers you. When you take initiative, you move from wishing to becoming. Be intentional, be courageous, and let your life reflect the vision that lives within you.

* * *

"Growth requires discomfort."

Growth is not always comfortable, but it is always worth it. Embrace the discomfort, for it is the path to transformation. Just as muscles grow through resistance, your spirit expands through challenges. Discomfort is not a sign of failure—it's a signal that you're evolving. Step into the unknown, face your fears, and trust that every stretch brings you closer to your highest self.

* * *

* * *

"Only through discomfort can you find growth and transformation."

Discomfort is the catalyst for change. Lean into it, and you will discover the transformative power of growth. The most profound lessons often emerge from the most challenging moments. When you allow yourself to sit with discomfort instead of fleeing from it, you unlock the strength, clarity, and resilience that were waiting within you all along. Growth is not found in comfort zones—it's discovered when you dare to go beyond them.

Afterword

As this journey of words comes to a close, the whispers of wisdom remain—echoing in the heart and mind, waiting to be revisited when the soul seeks clarity.

"Whispers of Wisdom: Quotes for the Soul" is not just a book to be read but a companion to be felt, reflected upon, and lived.

Each quote was written with the hope that it would reach you at the right moment, offering guidance, comfort, or a new perspective.

Life moves in cycles, and with every ending comes a new beginning. May these words continue to inspire you, reminding you that even in darkness, there is always light.

Thank you for allowing these whispers to become part of your journey. May you carry their wisdom forward, sharing it with the world in your own way.

With gratitude,

Samer

About the Author

Samer Merhi is a deep thinker and writer passionate about wisdom, philosophy, and personal growth. With a keen eye for life's hidden truths, he crafts thought-provoking reflections that inspire self-discovery and transformation. *Whispers of Wisdom: A Journey into the Depths of Truth* is his exploration of timeless lessons, offering readers a path to clarity and enlightenment.

Don't miss out!

Visit the website below and you can sign up to receive emails whenever Samer Merhi publishes a new book. There's no charge and no obligation.

https://books2read.com/r/B-A-CKIID-IQJYF

BOOKS2READ

Connecting independent readers to independent writers.